VIENNA BLOOD
& other poems

Also by Jerome Rothenberg

Poems

White Sun Black Sun   (1960)
The Seven Hells of Jigoku Zoshi   (1962)
Sightings I-IX   (1964)
The Gorky Poems   (1966)
Between Poems: 1960–1963   (1967)
Conversations   (1968)
Poems 1964–1967   (1968)
Poems for the Game of Silence   (1971)
Poland/1931   (1974)
A Seneca Journal   (1978)

Translations

New Young German Poets   (1959)
Hochhuth's "The Deputy," playing version   (1965)
Enzenberger's "Poems for People Who Don't Read Poems," with Michael Hamburger   (1968)
The Book of Hours & Constellations, or Gomringer by Rothenberg   (1968)
The 17 Horse-Songs of Frank Mitchell X–XII   (1970)

Anthologies

Ritual   (1966)
Technicians of the Sacred   (1968)
Shaking the Pumpkin   (1971)
America a Prophecy, with George Quasha   (1973)
Revolution of the Word   (1974)
A Big Jewish Book, with Harris Lenowitz and Charles Doria   (1977)

Recordings

From a Shaman's Notebook   (1968)
Origins & Meanings   (1968)
Horse Songs & Other Soundings   (1975)
6 Horse Songs for 4 Voices   (1978)
Jerome Rothenberg Reads Poland/1931   (1979)

JEROME ROTHENBERG

VIENNA BLOOD
& other poems

A NEW DIRECTIONS BOOK

ACKNOWLEDGMENTS

Grateful acknowledgment is made to the editors and publishers of maga-
zines and books in which some of the material in this volume previously
appeared: *Alcheringa, The Ark, Bad Breath, Bezoar, Boundry 2, Contact
II, Handbook, Inc., Isthmus, Montemora, New Directions in Prose and Po-
etry, New Wilderness Letter, Out of the West* (ed. Herb Yellen, Lord John
Books, Los Angeles), *Panjandrum, Poetry Review* (London), *River Styx,
So & So, Stations, Text, Tingpa* (Katmandu, Nepal), and *Zweitschrift* (Han-
over, Germany).

Portions of this book appeared as separate publications by Jerome Roth-
enberg and are reprinted here by permission of the publishers: John Mar-
tin and Black Sparrow Press (*The Cards*), Karl Young and Membrane Press
(*The Notebooks and Abulafia's Circles*), Walter Hamady and Perishable
Press (*A Poem to Celebrate the Spring & Diane Rothenberg's Birthday* and
B•R•M•Tz•V•H), and Katherine Kuehn and Salient Seedling Press (*Let-
ters & Numbers*).

Manufactured in the United States of America
First published as New Directions Paperbook 498 in 1980
Published simultaneously in Canada by George J. McLeod, Ltd., Toronto

Library of Congress Cataloging in Publication Data

Rothenberg, Jerome, 1931–
    Vienna blood & other poems.
    (A New Directions Book)
    (ND paperbook; 498)
    I. Title.
PS3568.086V5   811'.5'4   79–24966
ISBN 0-8112-0759-5

New Directions Books are published for James Laughlin
by New Directions Publishing Corporation,
80 Eighth Avenue, New York 10011

CONTENTS

1/Vienna Blood

THE STRUCTURAL STUDY OF MYTH

for Barbara Kirshenblatt-Gimblett

the thief became the rabbi
in that old story
others would say he was his father
all along   the way the moon
reflected in the water
is the water
maybe the master gonnif come to earth
old Trickster brother Jesus
didn't us Jews tell stories of his magic
"because we are like him"
the Crow Indian had said about Coyote
hitting the nail at last

AT THE CASTLE

seeing
its stone heart
the walls
are like walls
the gates like gates
& black
moon in the crook of tree
a yellow eye
it doesn't shine
the water dries against
my lips
o rainbow
will you fall?
o little heart
turn cold

.

tower.
broken.
every castle has.

.

night rises on
the valley
blanket on my bed

.

the child cries:
murder!
mushroom!
let them die with grace

·

A SCENARIO

for Richard Schechner

yiddish
vaudeville

is

fantastic
life

·

2000 people in the world
with mirrors

"THE JEW OF MALTA"

(1)

     Malta, Montana
     (let us say)
     with planks for streets
     sweet mornings
     smeared with horse shit
     the smell sticks to his nose
     so elegant he dreams
     back to a bride in Warsaw
     but his days
     are sad here dark
     the Jew is muttering
     sweeps out the sawdust to the street
     a gold ring gleams from

(2)

     I & Meester Meyer
     sit here with Sitting Bull
     & Red Cloud
     at the wop photographer's:
     Meester Meyer just a kid
     a dandy
     (dude)
     arrived here recently
     from Kansas (say)
     & spiks dee Eenglish
     he will sell you
     blankets boots sombreros levis swanky knives
     will take your daughters
     to his back room
     Meester Meyer
     he will raise their skirts
     & standing

on a stool will shtup them
harder harder
like foolish redskin
"what are Jews?"
asks Wyatt Burp
"but Injuns fresh arrived
"or not yet lost?"

(3)

the gentile model
to our likes
is ugly scans the hills
for gold
men screw the land
their armies
steal its people
blind
the boy with golden locks
(brave Custer)
rides his troops thru town
in Meyer's store he reads
sermons on poverty
the baptist chaplain blesses
soldiers heroes
gold flows down streams
the blood of Jesus flows
a soldier from his wallet pulls
vulva of squaw
his hand around it
squeezes
like an ancient baseball
like the heart of God

(4) BARRABAS'S SONG

"o my girl
"my gold my fortune my felicity

"o girl I do love o thee o thine
"so do I try to reach thee over distances
"the armies rise between us
"in the wounded bear they drive down
"main street   in his eyes you sit
"the soldiers laugh at us
"the Indians like Jews are in the hills
"the money here below
"therefore I do wait here still
"I practice thine enlargement
"I make sales at cost
"I steal the dreams of widows
"I speak the gentiles' lies
"their stink of empire I do smell
" 's like horse shit smeared on planks
"so I do wail for thee
"o girl   o gold   o beauty   o my bliss

SUTTER'S GOLD

for Scott McLean in Sacramento

"hot lizards" Sutter cries
rises from his bed
mattress stuffed with corn husks
"by Jo zis gold iss rich"
he says   his German sergeant
keeper of the keys
bows down
they rouse his honor guard
pure injun braves
snappy in blue drill pantaloons
white cotton shirts
red handkerchiefs twined round heads
or hung from branches
"my faithful servants"

Sutter writes
"on the advanced road to civilization"
while the others   native workers
sat at the feeding pans
ate the steaming wheat
with dirty hands
stuffed it down mouths
made farting noises
like flocks of cackling geese
or dug the beef out of the coals
& bolted it
ashes still adhering
some would escape back to the hills
were ever after
rounded up
like animals
he slapped their thick
vermin infested heads
he thrashed them
—communists & all—
the sand ran through the hour glass
the guard back of his room cried:
"all is well!"

THE ADVENTURES OF THE JEW

1

the Jew hero in each of us
hard man
man with the brutal appetite
swallows whatever waits
in his path
he has come by moonlight to a city
—call it Tunis

which puts it in the exotic east
or Waukesha
a little to the west of us—
there is a community of people there
who have lost touch with earth
they are without shadows in the sunlight
therefore they cry
like your mother's other children
born long before you
the strangers who invade your schoolyard
fair-haired demons
idiots
for whom the Jew must always be
the unfulfilled hero
they say:
this bread has no power to rise
call the Jew
the air is contaminated
water runs down hill
up hill
life has brought us to no real conclusions
only maladies
adjustments
days spent at work encompassed by
real saints or worse

2

      (a jewish anecdote)   one day a cry rose from the wed-
ding house   everything was ready   the guests were seated
    the hors d'ouevres were piled up in the kitchen   & the
orchestra was waiting   everybody's waiting for the bride
    & where's the bride   why there she is   she's climbing
up the stairs   she's starting to come through the door
    my god what agony   the door's a little low while she
    the bride   the lovely woman   is too large   she's
larger than the door   how will she get inside   what can
we do for her   we weary ourselves with huddles & discus-

sions   this is a disaster   should we renounce the bride
    should we smash the door   while everyone is at it
someone says   *call the Jew*   *only the Jew can rescue us*
from this disaster   someone goes looking for the Jew   he
arrives   he looks at the door   raises his clenched hands
    & brings them crashing down on the bride's head   the
bride says *ouch* while drawing her head in   he tells her
    go & enter now   people throw themselves on his neck
& hug him   someone showers him with gold

3

we have all called the Jew
whose lusts not intelligence
made him our hero
he who was last man at your wedding
found the others eating
his hands reached underneath the carpets
where the canned meats were set
his fingers in the fricassee
swam like arthritic dogs
the people cried:
what has become of the musicians?
is Moskowitz a jewish name?
why don't they dance at weddings any longer?
only the Jew can make them laugh
he does he cuts his fingers
at the second knuckle
a pinky drops into the bouillabaisse
eager for love he snaps
a crucifix in two
he eats the head & arms of Jesus
spits out the little bones
a voice caught in his throat
cries   Jesus
brother   jew   god
damn your soul
(he thinks)

next time you kill um
eat um up

4

  (a further anecdote) once the Jew traveled into a
country of yokels he passed by an orchard where he
spotted a stream of running water the day was warm
  he took out his handkerchief dipped it into the water
  washed his face with it hung it on the branch of a tree
  & stretched out in the shade he stretched himself out
for a siesta he fell asleep evening came but the Jew was
so tired he went on sleeping then the people came into the
city for the evening & the muezzin climbed the minaret of the
mosque to call them to prayer he turned from side to side
  & as he faced that tree in the shadow of which the Jew
was sleeping he said *my god* *the tail of the comet*
  & he began to cry *the tail of the comet* *the tail of*
the comet when they heard him the people ran around in
all directions weeping shouting *it's the end of the*
world *the tail of the comet has appeared* the noise
startled the Jew who woke up astonished & said *what's*
going on *they're saying that the world's in ruins* he
walked down to the city seeing the people in tears he asked
them *what's wrong* *has some catastrophe befallen you*
  they answered *don't you see* *it's the end of the*
world *the tail of the comet has appeared* the Jew raised
his head & saw that they were looking at his handkerchief
  which he had hung up in the tree & trembling he
told them *that's it huh* *tail of the comet huh* *what*
will you give me to get rid of it for you they said *what*
will we give you *why what will we give you* *we'll dress*
you up in gold *just lift this affliction from us* *that's all*
we ask of you he told them *stay right there* *don't*
budge then the Jew went out of the city he came to
the orchard examined his handkerchief to make sure it was
dry folded it in four put it in his pocket & came
back down he told them *see* *I've lifted this afflic-*

11

tion from you   the women looked at each other & uttered
cries of joy   the men embraced each other   & the Jew
     loaded down with all his heart desired   made his way to
Tunis   THEY'RE OUT THERE & WE'RE BACK HERE

5

the guests watch from the nearby hills
it is the Jew's turn now
mad Jew mad Savior
from whose beard hang fishes
victims of the storm
he dances backwards
to the gentiles' howls
is like a cowboy
dripping wet
who lifts the bride up to his lap
then forces her
over his iron cock
—o wonder of the ages—
how in love with me this people
will become (he thinks)
their faces remind him
of his mother's lambs
his father's involvements in the woods
o Tunis   Tunis
your awnings are the color of bright carrots
orphans ring your boulevards
with sheets
for water crying
"feed the dead"
they throw a cow's skull in your fires
when someone dies in Tunis
even the strangers call the Jew

COYOTE NIGHT POEM

1

at the edge of California sits
the dog man father
to his little wolves
"my children   babe & star
"my wormy offspring
let them go   he leaves
home & habitation
finds swamp to splash in
a marsh astride the sea
all night the birds
cross at his eyes they write
numbers in starlight
this dog man is obliged to read
& can't   no longer
his glasses tumble to the ground
to grope for to pick up
move the scene around
yourself the solid member
king of spectacles
he cries   the desperate convulsions
take on a color
blue red yellow
the small fly crawls along the floor
I speak   I say
"I would like to be a large fly"
he replies "no   small"
& time is like that
the small man becomes a fly
the dog becomes
a lady dog
the momma to his own pups
humble   senseless
the evidence is piling up
here on my table

"make the world sufficient
"for your praises
"the dog is too much with us
"night is day
"coyotes atop the supermarket
"read the signs
"they thwart their poisoners
this is the world of metamorphosis
you'd think
& change yourself
a turd would drop from you
a hundred black turds
to become a mountain
in your dream   beneath you
pushing you against the moon
pale lady   sliver
that which your mouth addresses
sliding moonbeams down your tongue
sky's belly cunt of heaven
—o illumination—
—glow—
"I am so hapless
"dog & man
"I dream this for my pleasure
"at edge of California
"in final splash
"of night
"I burrow for survival
"twice-born
"traveler
will grind his teeth against the earth
will beat it home

2

the scene is obvious: the man, appearing like a dog, is seated
in his dream: his feet rest in an old swamp, while his butt at
first is on a little hill: the man is no longer young & has trou-

ble seeing into his dream: he has lost his glasses, which mark
his kingship over the new landscape, & has to grope for them:
this adds to the sense of change & color & leads him to an
experiment in transformation, though not to his complete re-
lief: more than the fly which first attracts him, it's to his hid-
den female nature that he's drawn & a capacity for wolfish-
ness: motherhood is never easy but the night sky is & reminds
him that coyotes are the great transformers & survivers: he
repeats the archetypal defecation & light & buoyant rises to his
final love the moon: in the manner of cyclical comedy his feet
return him to an early dream

NOTES FOR A NEW WILDERNESS

1

I have escaped—she told him—
into the wilderness
But where is that?—he tried
to ask her—she was silent, never so silent as that day
she said: you could never track me there
—how be*wilder*ing—
it would be the last thought in his mind
I have—he said—my own road to walk
my own row to hoe
etc.
And the city sat above another city
which was its lost heart
its dark reflection
he thought: this is the wilderness
where she fled
& I can get there sooner, sooner or later
& he thought: no horizontal
geographies will do it
the new geography is up & down

like burial: from air
to earth
She must have thought long about
a new wilderness
it was she who named it
by living in it
& by reminding us
that everything is charted from the sky:
grey forms move over our heads
& force us down
& down
to find our terror
under the earth:
the mind, a little like that,
subtler
is also there
& lets us in
however sadly
to feel its pain—
he said that, then he said:
I cannot write a poem
—no longer—
only these notes

2   PREAMBLE TO A FLOOD

the world
waiting
to be washed away again
—the prophets tell us—
in the exhaustion of our language
too much talk
has emptied
too much writing ends it:
start of winter
on the road to Escondido
driving in the warm wind
the river—so sudden—opens to my eyes

almost in flood
a few dark orange trees
a white gate
houses down on the far side
—developments—
the money gone into developments
the interest in developments
a flood of paper
will change the landscape
—like the river—foreign now
direct the mind back to Allegany
more familiar ground
"a place almost like home"
but different: wilder
than beatings of the bear's heart
wildness we rouse
inside us
we are free to think about
to say: new savagery
translating from the French
who translate us
la nouvelle sauvagerie   (*for Jean Pierre Faye*)
& practice our wild system
—of talk & song—
that makes us poets:
language is the ground
we grow from—wild—
who has to look outside
to find it?
in us is darker colder
not heat of words
—blaze of reality—but buried
dead
unless you let it rise
or go down to its earth
o mystic brothers
in terror
there the new children stand around

17

a tree, forget
Coyote who escapes by shunning
poison—those who suffer
by their will
gone mad:
new wilderness   new death
new death   new road to zion

VIENNA BLOOD

for Herman Hakel

1

like carneval
for street & house
our action holds the place
between   the women
guard the door
no longer
they rush into the squares
& find
Vienna in the night
a jewless
hauptstadt city without
rime or grace
the others have survived in
alone   who stand
—friend Hakel—
muted cattle dumb
& lost
the darkness is their own
now   there is no one
can do again the thing
we did   the victim

dies
the mothers cannot
heal this birth
disorder of the town
where Hitler walked
he saw (sweet shadow) looming
the devil   Jew
my grandfather
this one could be
who scared him
shitless to Linz he ran
there buried
his face in the whipped cream
linzer torts
his momma saved for him
& roared
—o triumph of the will—
—disasters of the modern state—
the gentile's mind
is dumb & cruel
the song says
proven right

2   THE DANUBE WALTZ

I found a river
in Chicago
here I found one not
until the last day
on road to "airport"
saw it unwinding
saw it alongside
the left side
of the bus   how pale
& shy
thy houses
far from the architecture
built by empire

to its gods kings ministers of finance
waltzing
waltzing
in your grave
where is thy river
& thy woods
so old   like Jews
forever gone
we walk too among ghosts
the sounds of poetry
—ka ka—
the only music left us
arises still in Jandl's voice
a Jewish loaf still sold
at Neumarkt drowned out
still by waltzes
hokey
pokey
in shadow of thine arches
emperors have sat
the little cousins sit now
holding hands
the river (distant) waltzes on
to Budapest   between
thy left & right

3

the carnevals of middle
Europe blaze
the fetes bring
destroyers of a million worlds
to dance
by torchlight to punk rock
how heavy at night
their bodies are
& shine
their innocence is brutal

boots & belts
even the young ones wear
the artists
who carve crosses in their flesh
they lead us drunk
into Croatian bars
the German boy
sings Yiddish:
Rayzeleh
mine sheyneh
so jealous of
the sufferings of others
must inflict their own

4

the liminal   he writes
or "place between"
& sees   suddenly
the terror of that situation
terror in glass
in camphor
the eye inside his eye
looks back
finding the place he shades off
is not himself
now is not
some other self
insistent
feels like shit
& wonders:
at edge of what dark city
will he stop?
what phantom turning
that dark edge
also will stop
& stop him?
or Blake

"the draught of violence
"that draws extinction in"
uncertainty: a zone
a fruitful chaos
& the sacred's what's inside
the frame
(but what's inside it
if the terror
isn't there?
or what inside *me*
if I play the prince
in Nerval's tower
reading my poems in heart of
empty Europe
—luckless—
knowing too well these things
but hoping   like Artaud
"to break through language
"in order to touch life")
INSTRUCTIONS:
make a circle
around a tree
ring bells
cut sacred time out
live in it
a moment
doing everything
all senses
into play
be flexible
& playful
nothing fixed
but improvised
to name: all time all space
reversing roles
where all is open
—flowing—
the light shades off

the darkness
not yet complete

5

                                        for Victor Turner

communitas
(I meant to tell you)
is holy terror

NOTES TO "VIENNA BLOOD," ETCETERA

In August 1977 I spent a week outside Vienna, as one of two per-
formance artists (Performance Garage director Richard Schechner
was the other) at a Wenner-Gren Anthropological Foundation con-
ference on "ritual & performance." The setting was an old castle—
Burg Wartenstein—in a ruined tower of which I read & chanted
poems: an atmosphere charged by Victor Turner ideas of "com-
munitas" & "liminality" & by a sense of ghostly European histories,
the shadow of Hitler's home town (Linz) nearby, etc. In Vienna I
performed still more, thru friendly auspices of sound poet Ernst
Jandl & others, & wandered, once in drunk procession with young
artists/poets, thru that imperial but strangely voided city. Conversa-
tions with one Herman Hakel—a Jewish survivor—raised further
phantoms & horrors that colored the rest of the Vienna visit & even
the next week spent in still vigorous Paris (including French C. P.'s
huge Fête d'Humanité plus punk rock contexts everywhere). Vienna
stuck in my mind along with that title out of Johann Strauss's
Wienerblut, etc.

The Structural Study of Myth. Four brothers—rabbi's sons—rescue
the castle-locked king's daughter, mostly thru the youngest son: a
professional *gonnif* (thief) & locksmith. In the version Kirshenblatt-
Gimblett showed me, he turns down the kingship to become a rabbi.

"The Jew of Malta." Sketches for a play—version of Christopher

Marlowe's classic of same name—that Schechner & I did sometime speak of doing.

Sutter's Gold. After the Swiss Deutscher who founded Sacramento (CA) in the 19th century. Called it New Helvetia.

Adventures of the Jew. "Anecdotes" from Jewish Arabic versions; otherwise writ first of my winters in Milwaukee (1974–75).

New Wilderness. Name of my most recent magazine, which Jean Pierre Faye translated into French—a language that has no word for wilderness as such—as "nouvelle sauvagerie."

2/The Chicago Poem, & Others

FOR MICHEL BENAMOU (1929-1978)

les cloches sonnent sans raison
T. Tz.

how beautiful
the words seem:
how ridiculous at last
to fly there

in the wind
like ashes
dancing on the waves:
blue middle waters

l'eau te regarde
wrote Tristan Tzara
leaving a dull trace
seeds & mermaids

of the single
illness
we still nurture:
death

THE CHICAGO POEM

for Ted Berrigan & Alice Notley

the bridges of Chicago
are not the bridges of Paris
or the bridges of Amsterdam
except they are a definition
almost no one bothers to define
like life full of surprises
in what now looks to be the oldest
modern American city
o apparition of the movie version of
the future circa 1931
the bridges soon filled with moving lines
of people workers' armies
in the darkness of first December visit
along the water
bend of the Chicago River
the cliffs of architecture like palisades
at night the stars in windows
stars in the poem you wrote a sky
through which the el train pulls its lights
in New York streets of childhood
is like a necklace (necktie) in the language of
old poems old memories
old Fritz Lang visions of the night before
the revolution the poor souls
of working people we all love
fathers or uncles
lost to us in dreams & gauze
of intervening 1960s
there are whole tribes of Indians
somewhere inhabiting
a tunnel paradise
they will wait it out still
with a perfect assurance of things to come
everyone so well read in old novels
maybe the economics of disaster Ted
depressions of the spirit

so unlike the bright promise of
the early years
gloss of the young life easing death
atop a hill in Lawrence Kansas
the afternoon sky became aluminum
(illumination)
played on a tambourine to calm
the serpent fear
the material corpse that leaves us vulnerable
everyone will come to it I think
I do not think you dig it
getting so out of hand so far away
but we remain & I will
make another visit soon
hope we can take a walk
together it is night & we are
not so bad off have turned forty
like poets happy with our sadness
we are still humans in a city overhung
with ancient bridges
you pop your pill I laugh
look back upon the future of
America & remember
when we both wrote our famous poems called
Modern Times

A POEM TO CELEBRATE THE SPRING & DIANE ROTHENBERG'S BIRTHDAY

3/20/75

.   .   .   .   .   .

in celebration of your day
a birth day
which also is spring the equinox

a quarter's separation from my time near
the winter solstice
hunter in my own head
(candle candle)
of the ram in thicket
fisher in pools of Hebron
you between the water & the sky
memory of our bodies in the water
summer night we found
deserted beaches in Virgin Islands
(who was a virgin then?)
the stars ran through our hands
like gods we walked
our story written in celestial alphabets
bright alephs
burnt in my mind or yours
a message   you will live
forever you will never die

.   .   .   .   .   .

2

what if the memory starts at
this point like a sound
the unspeakable god contracted to a breath
endures   extends   is taken
into aether
doesn't die
the way that an angel speaking
speaks an angel
into life
o logos
material reproduction of the gods
the function of whose worshippers
through song
is pleasure   paradise
I move inside you
(you in me)
the continuity is so intense

death only interrupts it
briefly

. . . .

3

back to the Bronx it travels
with us
how could I know you were
the most amazing
girl with massed hair of 1946
the New Year
myself with pompadour
struggled with steps I hardly knew
still counted numbers
whether as dance or poem o fox trots rhumbas sensations of
     the lindy
in living rooms too tight for
conversations
crowds of children
all come back to mind
when summoned
hallucinations or wet dreams
mysteries still out of reach
were like countries to be traveled
houses to be lived in
"doubt" the voice says "a condition"
nearly 30 years beyond
first choice of my childhood
whether to go on living
as I wanted
but was always afraid death would call me back
for which we curse
fathers   mothers
who placed us on the wheel
we who turn the wheel ourselves
turn it into birth
not knowing
knowing if it's better

to have been born or not
that only a small light takes us through
the darkness   nature of the universe
death that can make a mystery of love

. . . . . .

(an old poem)

THE MAIDEN

                  I would sing of
who is daughter of light   on whom
brightness of kings does rest
I would delight in her image's rays
her beauty   whose garments
are flowers sweet odors rise from
a king looks out from her eyes
will feed those beneath him
in truth   truth covers her head
the tread of her feet brings pleasure
she spreads her lips open
for beauty   sings praise poems
32 singing her praises
tongue like a curtain the priest can raise up
& enter   her neck mounts high
like a staircase   first builder hung there
her hands that were speaking
in code   led the dance of the aeons
fingers that opened the gates
to the city   whose chamber
vibrates with light
the odor of sweet leaves & myrrh
strewn with branches of myrtle   sweet flowers
a door decked with reeds
stand the seven who guarded the groom
whom she chose   seven bridesmaids
who dance for her praise her
twelve more by her count who are servants
attend her   their gaze
toward the bridegroom

sighting of whom brings them light
of the joy of their entry
those who would be at that marriage
assemblage of princes   long feasting
long lives of those given to life
wore garments of light splendid raiment
would swoon in their joy in praise of
father of all   take his light down
exult in it   light of their vision
of godlight
sweet food now received
sweet perfection sweet drink
of his wine   ends thirst   desire
bursts into praises o breath
o father of truths o mother of knowing

B·R·M·Tz·V·H: A poem from memory for Matthew
Rothenberg's 13th birthday celebrated as a "bar mitzvah
event" one month after the date three decades three years
past my own

．　．　．　．　．　．

naming the day it comes
deep into March
Aquarius has shifted into Pisces
—Diane's time—
waters receded & warm days
hanging over San Diego
where never in my life I thought to end up
or thought to be here
standing in this western yard
to make bar mitzvah
as event—I stress—not
the ghost of ceremony
I recall from my own lost 13th year

middle of wartime & reports
first coming in that told
deaths of others curly-headed
cousins sacrificed
only their photos left to scan thru
later • "who is this?"
you asked
"a child" I answered
hair curled like your own
forget it
death's depressing after all
someone still dreams of
a universe   benign   & wakes
to stifled flesh
I wouldn't interrupt this day with
but wonder
how any sanity was possible
this century
o Matthew Matthew born once
in the glow of brother—Milton's—death
the mystery thus thrust
into our thoughts
—of light & dark
co-equals—
I was alone to greet you (as I hope
you will not be)
of those who shared the table
at our home back in the Bronx
by then I was
the one surviving
(as I knew it would be)
& thought: how could I
bring them to life for you
except the poems pictures
I began around
their deaths   your life
fathers mothers grandmothers
set there as titles
ancestors the imagination made
the shades all poetry

recalls back to Ulysses in the pit
voice of David out of Sheol
orphic Jew my master
de profundis I could see her wraith
—those mad poetic words!—
my mother enter in dark of
restless sabbaths
she who would call us "sweet face"
too much love
has spoiled her
I could never
answer that or answer
my father's angers
disappointments of his life in dry goods
peddling peddling
the old books forsaken
he dropped off in sleep & told me
"strange that it takes so long to die"
& she "the whole town's talking"
mysteries of death
& life
fantastic faces all we know
we love
bar mitzvahs happening
on sabbaths that divide
the day that Jesus died
from Easter
—Esther of my mother's name—
when all the dead arise
in mind they sing
song that first ushered in your birth
a man child   son
grown old & beautiful
at last
"joy   joy
"praise   praise

FOR BREYTEN BREYTENBACH IN PRISON

. . . . . .

far now from Rotterdam
& the small talk of poets   mouths
devouring little fishes
freed of the metaphor inside the act
knowledge of the world that if we face it
drives us mad
o Breyten vision of schizophrenia
is gnostic truth
division of world along its axis
of split in consciousness
sickness that doesn't heal itself it is
the way of the beginning raises
in the mouth a cry
will bring it to the light
o light
how can I think of all these friends in prison
like the world itself
(poor world)
& wonder at my safety
walk with Homero in the streets of London
with Jean-Clarence in Paris
last week where we spoke of you
Breyten Breytenbach who sat with us
a year ago that other summer
asked my son to write a poem
greet the poets of the world in Rotterdam
o poets poets
we are all split for love
of woman   of the world
the severed being searches out
its contrary   as skin
as color   cannot move too fast
but tries an assemblage for the friends
a gift of language offered
we who should withhold our speech

in anguish
should share the silence God brings on the world
each in our little corner
destiny
as Shakespeare in mouth of Lear
"but let me not go mad"
why not?
the mind spins out its images
alone   the music of
another evening now reborn
the Red Fanfare plays on the stage
a crazy march song
poets of the world
united
in vision of our common death
with all the prisoners
weird fish who eat the fish
are eaten by the fish
the tiny silver bodies
of our flesh itself in witness
to a proposition
revolution makes us what we are
o poets
minds whose minds turn upside down
revive the oldest maddest dream
a word called freedom

FROM "THE NOTEBOOKS"

9/75

(1)

not hell's brilliance
butterflies that sting
stung us into vision
but as here

illumination of the mind
is from the upper worlds
their hell mere ugliness
so that
the pain of vision
terror
finds its place in heaven
although it blinds the eye

(2)

I never knew heaven
could be terrible as hell
or be as bright

.   .   .   .

9/75

a letter to Nathaniel Tarn   to honor *lyrics for the bride of god*   at this point in the writing

.   .   .

& seeing the old struggle there
—even in God the Androgyne   division
conflict of the sexes
later would pull the world apart—
the mind evades it   almost
smug in the male imagination builds a house for her
or sets her up in it
the House of God
though if it's HIS house or if it's HER house who could say
       now?
as the other day a letter from our old friend Clayton came
"that the Shekinah is just another one of the 'masks' that male
       origin wears"   he wrote
—I wouldn't doubt it for a minute either

though   that adjustment made   the question will still
     remain
of domicile   of building that greater world
that replication of the *shi'ur koma*
& the mind   the mind will ache from it forever
throbbing   call it   habitation
call it palace   "image of the world"   they said
& wrote about the heavens
seven by their count
now I have read the *hekhalot* the books of palaces
before Shekinah   GOD THE MOTHER   in her exile
sat outside the town & heard the trains call
like voices of her angels
she who first experienced the *galut* poor old soul

.   .   .   .

10/75

for Kafka
dying in the cold
I said
come in come in
—we could have been together
he the poet was a friend the one who gave us
that image of Amerika
but writing out of Prague—
the law of worlds
no the made law of the world we know
descends on him
splinters the skull
poor brains & lungs spill out
as we are only meat upon the earth
but lovers
sometimes voices
rise in us we didn't know
o Kafka
take me one step further in the book
who wrote his father

taunted with visions of what crazy torah
as a child
when they would open up the ark
"reminds me of the shooting galleries
"where a cupboard door would open
"in the same way
"anytime you got a bullseye
"only with the difference
"something interesting would come out there
"but here
"the same old dolls
"& headless
called it torah also
in the darkness
stood before the law
we whispered
visions
of faces
messengers
who came for him
the silent
sons of god

.   .   .   .   .   .

10/75
a letter to Meltzer for his 3rd visit to Milwaukee

how you first came
will come the day after these words
are written
typing your poem of *Hero/Lil*
reading it again
I wonder
what this *zeitgeist* is
drives us still to believe in "chance"
that brings you when my thoughts are bound
with yours
your name has called you

—that would have been the magic once—
you David singer thru your father's side
but thru the mother's too
wonders of the old books we both read
those martyrs to the images
mad Jews whose words
splintered the ONE into di-
versity who
robbed of freedom
dreamed it back to life
high spirits   friends
as you saw Lilith
equal woman
power in the earth
o good & evil still
persisting
a poetry of changes
as the Zohar tells us
THERE IS SAMAEL
& THERE IS SAMAEL
& THEY ARE NOT THE SAME

.   .   .   .   .   .

11/75
(a dream)

                                    in memory of Wallace Berman

the Alphabet came to me
in a dream
he said
"I am Alphabet
"take your light from me
& I thought
"you are numbers first before you are sound
"you are the fingers' progression & you end in the fist
"a solid mass against the world
but the Alphabet was dark
like my hand writing these words
he rose

not as light at first though issuing from light
but fear a double headed body
with the pen a blacker line at center
A began it but in Hebrew not a vowel
a choked sound it was the larynx stopped the midrash said
     contained all sound
sound of Alphabet initial to all speech
as one or zero
called it WORK OF CREATION in my dream
a creature more than solid more than space or distance
& he said
"all numbers & all sounds
"converge here
but I knew it   said
that I would count my way
into the vision
grooved thus with numbers & with sound
the distances to every side of us
as in a poem

. . . .

11/75
for Armand Schwerner   as introduction to a series of poems
about the world   earth foremost in our thoughts

the way the words come
"down to earth"
as if to signal passage
that we leave the world where mind breathes purely
& come down to find
again materials
a space that comes up solid
to my hand
o matter matter
consciousness is also touch
creation is creation of this place
image of what we are
life felt most sharply where the dead wait

where our fathers do not sleep
do not not-sleep
earth that the book has led us down to
will show the way home at last
a world of obstacles
—"that crush me" Kafka wrote—
in beautiful pursuit
procession into sun moon stars
the tree outside the house becomes
the road to heaven
shamans climb it with our children
fathers did too
whose beards tangled in its branches
animals & people in a world we knew
soon to be wrested from us by invasion
of some darker mind
knowledge by which we named our animals
or named ourselves
for animals
a language shared
pleasures
fulfillments
in a world of nouns

. . . .

12/75
a letter to Paul Celan in memory

of how your poems
arise in me
alive
my eye fixed on
your line
"light was • salvation"
I remember
(in simpler version)
Paris
nineteen sixty seven

in cold light of
our meeting
shivered to dumbness
you said "jew"
& I said "jew"
though neither spoke
the jew words
jew tongue
neither the mother language
loshen
the vestiges of holy speech
but you said
"pain"
under your eyebrows
I said "image"
we said "sound"
& turned around to
silence   lost
between two languages
we drank wine's words
like blood
but didn't drink toward
vision   still
we could not speak
without a scream
a guttural
the tree
out of the shadow of
the white café was not
"the tree"
roots of our speech
above us
in the sun
under the sewers
language of the moles
"who dig & dig
"do not grow wise
"who make no song
"no language
into the water silence

of your death
the pink pale sky of Paris
in the afternoon
that held no constellations
no knowledge of the sun
as candelabrum
tree   menorah
"light knotted into air
"with table set
"chairs empty
"in sabbath splendor
the old man stood beside
in figure of a woman
raised his arms to reach
axis of the world
would bring the air down
solidly
& speak no sound
the way you forced
my meaning
to your poem
the words of which still press
into my tongue
"drunk
"blesst
"*gebentsht*

3/The Cards

Several years ago I entered into a poetry game with Bernadette Mayer, Ed Friedman & seven other poets & artists. We each selected a commercial postcard & sent a copy to the other participants, who then responded with a poem or art piece about each card, their own included. Among the cards were pictures ranging from a sexy turn-of-the-century Italian lady with a blazing red ball in her outstretched hand; a photo close-up of volcanic fires at Mount Etna; a long-distance shot of an irrigation canal in Red China; a group of antique American paperweights, etc. My own selection was a picture of an old Indian couple whom I knew from living at the Allegany Seneca Reservation in Salamanca, New York, & whom the others of course did not know. The game (which had a second, more complex part) was never completed, but in the effort to make sense of what I was given, I found the process no different from that of any other poem.

THE CARDS (I)

My
Red Etna
Mask
In
Yellow
Is bird inside
My yard
Whose friend's red
Car
Sits
Idles
In sunlight
's green tomatoes
Sadly
Ripen
In his mind
Red
Etna
Savage
Sausage
Cook um up

THE CARDS (II)

Is lady who holds
A ball
She's momma my sweet
Lady
On whose fingers red is
Blood
This ball's her breast
A red hot melon
Maybe

Or maybe Momma Sunlight
Is a dancer kid
Whose light's a red hot bauble
Etna flames again
Called "Edna"
Thy name means pleasure & delight
Like Eden
Ishtar
Star
Her white hair flies from
Head
She prophesies
A kingdom
& the smudge covers the card
Cerises ou sang
My esoteric darling
Pink thy flesh is in the light
Of suns against
My own thighs
Breasts
Green the clouds form
Back of her
"Mine lady riseth from the sea
"O lady who holds all worlds inside thine hand
Jut of thy jaw
I love
Thy red hot immies
Shall I not now speak thy name good
Make it ring clear in
Greek or Italian

THE CARDS (III)   "Moon"

Lunatic
Rock

How would I know the moon was blue
Like the face of the blue god
Krishna whom everybody now knows
I didn't guess the skin would be that blue
Cerulean
The color of his ice blue madness
Blue men walk through
Under a black sky
Lunatics
& moon men—
Mocking the female principle wherever they go
The goddess the pink lady
Plays with fire
Holding the red orb flames of hot Etna
In her hand
She denies cold love
Opens the crater of her volcanic cunt
To seize him
The blue rocks of the moon sucked
Into hot momma's belly
Captive
They screw his blue brain into place
One blue note
Shivers loose
Blue of his moon mouth fills the glass
Color of his death

THE CARDS (IV)   "Nude Dunes"

Movie of
Earth fuck
How heavy the cock appears
Black in the photograph
Imagined
Red or blue

A blood dream in the sand
Of shadows
Ridges = ribs
Depressions = flesh
The flexed leg in the corner
= what?
A flexed leg
Hill of sand
Finely the warm grains spread across
The film
& the eye that holds the aperture
Fills with emotion
Dare we say red flame?

THE CARDS (V)   "Paperweights"

1

First had come
To a flower
First had come
& a flower
Spotted first
But a flower
But leaf & lily
One a flower
Rose & strawberry
& once a flower
Clouds or vortices
Like a flower
& so lights & verticals
& so like a flower

2

was crystal
& crystal

& was crystal
& crystal was
& yellow
& blue
& green
& yellow
& red
& blue
& yellow
& was crystal
& crystal
& crystal was
& was crystal

3

Sweet william
& more sweet william
& circling
Sweet & william
Red
& yellow
& sweet william
& more
more & four
& five
& four
& more
& nine
& nine
& more
Therefore before
& more
& circling
& more sweet william

4

Dare we say apple

Dare we say apple core
& blue
& dare we say blue
& blue sand
Dare we say sand
& flame
One a red flame

5

Flower & white
Snow & snow white
Red & delight
Blue & just right
Eyes that shine at night
Eyes at night
Eyes night
& fishes somewhere bright
Seen by fish light

THE CARDS (VI)   "Red Flag Canal"

Seen by fish light
Of fish seen at a wall in
China
At Red Flag Canal
The ground is fish wet
The woman in a pink & blue shirt
If imagined blue
Looks toward the hills in blue light
Her shirt reveals the male & the female principles
Of Tao & Mao
She feels her skin cool in the rain
She is the rain herself

She thinks
"The Others
"Walking the wall above
"Red Flag Canal
"Are the embodiments of my own delight
"In China
"Wet walls & red fish
"Pagodas blue veined
"Suicides
"The contrary corners of whose minds converge
"In perfect dialectic

THE CARDS (VII)   "Bird of Paradise"

Like the woman herself
The bird of paradise
Is Eden
Edna's bird
Their colors are like the labia of volcanoes
What we achieve
Only by disease
The festering wound
Translucent
They are born to
& die
For the love of red
For plumage
In numbers of up to 80,000 males
They crumble
Their 80,000 yellow & green necks
Wrung dry
How different they seem from
The lowly crow
Their brother
Maybe the only bird of hell

THE CARDS (VIII)   "Untitled"

1   A bird finds a tree
    & a cloud

2   A bird in a tree
    & a cloud

3   A tree
    & a cloud

4   A bird
    & a cloud

5   A bird in five
    & a cloud

6   A bird not six
    & a cloud

7   A cloud
    & a cloud

8   &
    & a cloud

THE CARDS (IX)   "The Diviner"

That couple sitting
In splendor of old houses
Albert Jones & his wife Geneva
Were old before my time
He was

The last of the Seneca diviners
Died 1968
Year we first stayed in Salamanca
With the power to know dreams
"Their single divinity" wrote Fremin (S.J.) 1650
As we say "divine"
The deva in us
Like a devil
Or a divus (deus)
When these old woods were rich with gods
People called powers
They would appear in words
Our language hides them
Even now
The action of the poem brings them to light
Dear David
Not in the business man's
Imagination
But asking
Who is Edna?
Forces them out of the one mind
To surface in our tongues
In mything
Mouthing the grains of language
As David that sounds like Deva
Means beloved
Thus every Indian once had a name

This poem, in a slightly altered version, appeared in *A Seneca Journal* (New Directions, 1978).

"In perfect dialectic
"The two great Chinese pandas
"Tao & Mao
"Could be considered as
"The male & the female principles
"Were nicknamed Yin & Yang

4/Letters & Numbers

. . . .

once it turned
twice darkly
thrice was more than they could stand

—more like their shadows—
& there was no word for four:
three was enough

ALEPH POEM

for David Meltzer

in peace the aleph
rises: on bishop's hat
the aleph rests

•

aleph & a dog
are friendly

•

as the masked man stumbles
to the street
a windpipe bursts
words & letters pour out
on the pavement

•

alephs sit beside a truck

•

sound before a sound
is spoken: aleph

•

the tear inside a tear

TRISTAN TZARA

(*an acrostic*)

try rumania in sunlight
try a napkin

try zanzibars
and real alarmclocks

try ruins icebergs snails
try april nuns

try zealously
arks ravens anchors

NUMEROLOGY

(a)

the man of numbers
cries too loud
he is a cipher   empty
his spaces
are yours
they open up through him
a cloud & sky
beyond him
centered in the holes they make
I call out
1!
2!
7!
9!
falling against his shadow
on the rock

(b)

9–9
shadow
rock
1
7–7–7–7–7
shadow
1
shadow cipher sky
1
spaces
9–9
shadow
9
numbers
9
1–1–1–1–1
2
cipher
empty
2
yours
2
shadow rock
9
7–7–7–7–7
sky
shadow sky
sky cloud
1 cloud
7 cipher
hole
7 hole
9 hole
shadow hole
1 spaces
cipher
cipher
1
7

empty
7
number

NUMEROLOGY   "A Song"

One
Number one
And one
And a one
A.
And an A
A A A
And a three
Three & C
A & B
Into three
And four
Into D
Into G
B & E
Minus three
Minus D
And me
And divided by me

GEMATRIA   "The Goddess"

Shekinah (1)

100.

Shekinah (2)

My light.

Shekinah (3)

O light me.

Shekinah (4)

X.

SEVEN GEMATRIA

(1)

A Tree

A woman.

(2)

Earth

Heart.

(3)

Star

River.

(4)

Sungod

Snake.

(5)

Sun

Moon on moon.

(6)

Moon

Man.

(7)

Woman

Moon.
Moon.
Moon.
Moon.

A POEM FOR *AYIN*

young girl reminds me:
write a poem
for *ayin*

this is it!

ayin: pharyngeal stop, 16th letter of the Hebrew alphabet

FOUR ACROSTICS

(henri chopin)

hollow
electric
nuance
rains
inside

controlled
he
opens
proud
ionic
nuts

(bob cobbing)

by
our
breath

circles
of
blue
brilliance
illuminate
nature's
gloom

(ernst jandl)

ernst
reads
new
songs
tonight

just
as
known
delights
linger

(jackson mac low)

joy
and
curious
kin-
ship
of
no-one

more
accurate
cranky

logical
or
wild

AIRPLANE POEM   "The Circles"

(Í)

circles on the earth
—somewhere in Kansas—
what do they mean?
I take the circular form to mark
the coming of Messiah
day by day

—but not in Kansas!—

(2)

Farmers plow in circles

Is it true?
I can't believe it!

From the air I honor
their circles on the earth

A poet:
the instincts of a little god

(3)

the earth of Kansas
is America's
enduring work of art

TIRED BODY. TIRED LETTER.

for Edmond Jabès

the death before the death
the death after

two deaths
like signal & response

like whispered time
to witness

what's on your mind
what's inside

eye & empty eye
a mirror

a common door

NOTES TO "LETTERS & NUMBERS"

I was drawn back—while in the process of constructing *A Big Jewish Book*—the "gematria" (numerology) sections in particular—to a consideration of number as it enters our works & lives. A "poetry of number" (& for the Jews all letters of the alphabet were numbers, each page a field of numbers) was once the limit of the poetry we could see, not only that "numbers" was itself the working term for "verse," but that it linked *all* arts & sciences together: a great unifying & synthesizing concept with roots into the Orphic-based, inspired & sacred mathematics of the Pythagoreans. Wrote Aristotle, who was no way at ease with it:

> The Pythagoreans were . . . the first to take up mathematics. . . . & thought its principles were the principles of all things. . . . Since they saw that the modifications and ratios of the musical scales were expressible in number; since, then, all other things in their whole nature seemed to be modelled on numbers, & numbers seemed to be the first things in the whole of nature, they supposed the elements of all things, & the whole heaven to be a musical scale & number.

And above their heads the stars grouped themselves into letters, numbers, appearing thus to the literate but still luny wanderer of the Zohar, he who looked out to the east, there saw "something like letters marching in the sky, some rising, others descending. These brilliant characters . . . the letters—numbers—with which God has formed heaven & earth."

For myself the numbers have been a presence beneath speech, but I have known them also, being Jewish, in the letters of the alphabet I work with. My father drew them with his finger on the kitchen table. And I have lain awake like him & counted numbers in sequences that play on mind & body until the rhythm of numbers, letters, shapes, & forms is inescapable—as still another source of naming.

Aleph Poem. First letter of the Hebrew alphabet; & behind the "Aleph Poem" a memory of its use, along with other Hebrew letters, by the West Coast artist Wallace Berman.

Acrostics for Chopin, Cobbing, Jandl, & Mac Low. Written at the "Sound & Syntax International Festival of Sound Poetry," Glasgow, Scotland, May 1978.

Gematria. Traditional Hebrew letter-number coding practice transposed to English. Numerically equal words are juxtaposed, the combinations read for "meaning."

Tired Body. Tired Letter. Title quoted from Jabès's lecture-essay, "The Question of Displacement into the Lawfulness of the Book."

5/Abulafia's Circles

A POEM IN YELLOW AFTER TRISTAN TZARA

(Invocation):

angel slide your hand
into my basket   eat my yellow fruit
my eye is craving it
my yellow tires screech
o dizzy human heart
my yellow dingdong

ABULAFIA'S CIRCLES

. . . .

1

the master of the book
of lights
he points to them
& back again
to you
the letters lead his hand
he lets them
flicker
proud & sensual
he makes a star between his thumb
& pointer
crying for a fish
asks the sea to beat less
takes a journey
to the stars
& back
a sentimentalist
his tongue once licked the fingers of
the pope
he sleeps late
often
in the city of Salonika
dines on baklava
(tra la)
or sleeps with sleep
he calls her
"cousin"
"shepherdess"
the hole inside his room leads
down to another room
the room leads to a hole
under the rock

is water
"I am the water in the rock"
he sings
& hears the traffic
music of Jerusalem
o tambourines
o phantoms
mechanics dance for him
how can he light the lights
or douse them
but puts his lips against the candle
speaks to it
an "e" drops from his mouth
& freezes
like voice in comic strips
the words are
circles
Abulafia & Hannah Weiner
face to face
"I came here to New York
"I crossed Sambation
"I heard the stones cry
"the thunder sing
"I saw the naked bodies of the storm
"with holes
"with letters
"I became a clock
"I was the moon
"I quavered
"letters were on my wrists
"you read them
"letters were on the moon
"the oven
"I counted with your fingers
"I was dumb
"the moon over the gasworks
"red eye
"blue lantern

"words like bees
—a crowd assembles—
"words like lips"
it surges in his mirror
multiples of ten
o gloss
o lexicon
"my vowel-pointed hand
"with palm for measure
"calms them
"ABULAFIA they cry to me
"don't give it a moment's thought I say
"seeing there's danger all around
"the city frees its daughters
"teases me
"with dreams   the pen of G-d
"spells MAFIA
—prophetic rhyme!—
"he steps out of the candle
"he is Bugsy Siegel
"little Bugsy
"on his arm Virginia Grey
"waves to the lens
"my mirror holds them like
"a circling sword
now comes a month of deals
Las Vegases rise up
over Amerika
the gentile landlord howls
the hit man—
strapped in his vest—
leers from the auto
Europe's daughter
grimaces
"we will take you prisoner"
they say
the saintly tramp
G-d's child

wild in his derby
brimless
wants to escape
the door against
his fringes
grips him
he'll watch the scene develop
blood on the lens
—is it life or just
another movie?—
o film life is fantastic
night is day
the life of Fritz the Kat
the life of Edgar Kayce
proves Kabbalah
"o mine lehrer   *o my teacher*
"bruder   *brother*
"kummt mit mir tsum tish   *come to my table*
"ah khaseneh shtellt for   *a wedding's underway*
"esst fish   *eat fish*
"esst reytekher   *eat radishes*
"belibter   *beloved*
(end of dialogue)
the poem goes on
however   Hannah Weiner
fades with gangland
I who take the trains
thru Europe
on whom Vienna stares
again   the braided
breads
armpits of our brides
are in all windows
in all shops
the tongue goes brrrrk
it licks the egg white
surface   tighter
sighs her voice

74

the crumbs lodge in the teeth
of wise man   shaman
Abulafia who travels
fast down the jew street
turns the corner
where Hitler turned
I see him
I dream of Hitler now
myself o false Jew
"man of enterprise
(he mocks me)
"dirty you are
"needing soap
"these people are so dirty
"(pheh)
"I Hitler Shitler
"smelling so smartly of wagnerian highs
"so beautiful my little
"artist's hands
"I curse out Dada
"freaks who scrub not
"I am pure
"like Viennese confections
"no Slav I but the fairest Deutscher
"confronting here
"visage of this monster
"he who counts
"wrong making 2 plus 2
"be *five*
thus spoken only thus
the power of his eye
his sour lip
clears out Vienna in
an eye wink
empty   even Abulafia
no Jewish buddies here shall find
but she deserted
blind herds of the dead

around her rings
her circles
city   city
"this is the prophecy
"say I I Hitler
he replies o you
o Hitler I messiah Abulafia
am bound to you
in history
where vowel calls to vowel
our paths have crossed
you kill I bring them
back to life
G-d's double nature shines thru us
your left hand
holds my right
the name each calls
is other
male & female
I & you
over your eyeballs flutters
the face of little Eva
mother   daughter
to us all
—o Jacob Frank—
—o Juan Peron—
each of us so incomplete
so partial
lacks the totality
the myth lays claim to
& the male
most partial impotent
seeks life
out of his own body
the skull splits first from migraine
from pain of intellect
he lies there
in back of the hut he pushes

knees to his chest
compresses the sphincter & expands
to bursting
thus the prophecy: messiah
giving birth
dance of the colored winds
& lights
who move like gentile phantoms
letters erupting
sparking from the walls
they rise & fall in rhythm
to his labors
while the roof is
set in motion
within the place called Bird's Nest
spins around him
as he reaches for the rings
at center of the carousel
the letters sing o Abulafia
whose meanings
fail us
flowers spun from
the four colors of the glow
colors of the alphabet
he leaves a babe behind him
will transpose that dream
to paper   circles
everywhere
the bodies mass around the flame
begin the round dance
& explode
red alephs
yellow yods
blue hum of ayins
the mystical poetry of our own time
on loops of tape
white noise that contains
all colors

"what you hear-see
"I speak-show
"what I write
"you learn to witness
"no longer split
"no longer speech that isn't
"written on flesh
we celebrate
all nature writes us
the small beasts spill their seed
on walls
our sperm draws letters on
the belly of the bride

. . . .

2 THE SECRET DREAM OF JACOB FRANK

> "So in Poland for the first time I did things which no
> one knows   for these were things which the lips
> cannot utter   The heart keeps them to itself"
> —J.F., *The Sayings of the Lord*

remembered
he is your counterpart   the other
Jew transgressor
of their law
moves to the performance of
your dream
the synagogues he stalks thru
scrolls thrown down
this madman   nihilist
once mounted
pissed 'gainst the parchment
howling
he would lisp in mockey yiddish
banged shutters

where our wise men—sages—slept
"I am the crow"
(he cried)
"the cock in frenzy
"will fly past Reno
"to my wedding
"secrets of the faith lead me
"to the Queen of Germany
"her Jews will plot against me
"screams will follow
"when I leave her
"far off in time
"remembered in prison
"I am a simple man
"delaying
"stood me on the table
"saw the abyss below
"fell thru to it
but wakened
further off the lady
lingered
mad astrologer
her body danced to his
all night
kept waking
making entrances
"again I meet you mistress
"in Bohemia
"the clocks are cookoo here
"the floors of bedrooms
"shine with hearts
"the ceilings
"painted with red hearts
"& heart-shaped mirrors
"near your bed
"so slavic like the maids
"who feed us
"I messiah Jacob Frank

"am in the center of
"a giant heart
"my member raised to strike
"thee my shekinah bride
"on eiderdowns
"thou leans to me
"thy mouth is like a birdcage
"—lock me up in it!—
"& swallow floods of love
"like chicken drippings
"passed from mouth to mouth
"the tongue of me messiah Jacob Frank
"is on the tongue of thee
"Shekinah Lilith Lady of the North
he said   like simple man
had brought two ladders to her roof
& climbed them
Queen Shekinah looks down
from her painted cloud
her heavens filled with horses
he can mount
the door into her bosom
opens   closes
riding the sky the sun
is now a man
he stares at you then turns
back to the lady
they will fly off together
waving *la*
dee da they sing
the advent of Italian opera
stirs the cantors
dirty songs become
G-d's words
my little honey girl
—he sings &
hugs the torah—
I am raw with love

& catch you
by the river I will snatch
your books
will walk beside the shores
150 wagons
wait on
for the simple man
robe bundled on his head
who swims across
jeering faces of Rumanians
abuse him
their corn mush weighs him down
"sweet Jews."
(he says)
"my journey is my own
"my dreams are thin
"o little g-d
"the image of my lady floats still
"over head
"she sister to the sun
"will lend a horse to me
"crosswise from channel
"I have sprung
"to land in Bukavina
"home of thieves
"in spades
"in diamonds
raises his fists
with cards hard at the flush
cut gems whose value
no one knows
our leader!
say the thieves
our little g-d!
& welcome him
around their fires drinking
their sour wines
now tells his visions:

armies of Jewish gonnifs
march with him
on roads to Warsaw
the women sing
a queen steps forward
she leaves the gentile crowd
to give him
hand of his daughter once again
wise one she calls him
master jew
he beats his drum hard
daughter & shekinah become one
beside him in his wagon
—hauled by demented bears—
but the lovers
speak in Polish   Turkish
is their second tongue
the gentiles stand in awe
sounds of entwining serpents
in their ears
their wallets lined with stone
caverns of metropolis appear
trains like comets
down its streets
the wagon moves beneath the "el"
to make a living
they will sell new knives
to wives & daughters
"o the lives of Jews are hard"
(the song goes)
"even the messiah sits
"in shit
"beside the sewers   screws
"an eye toward heaven
lady fades
the sun in darkness shuts
his only lid
box buried in the earth

her catholic angels sing
"hosanna"
in the speech of mice

. . . .

3 THE HOLY WORDS OF TRISTAN TZARA

sad in his world
or in yours
he walks for years beside
the economic lilies
explores the mysteries of bread
a wax archangel
stands on his tongue
his hands   cold   dry
deprived of water
in the room under the room
where Lenin sat
aromas of Bukovina gather
Moinesti with its corn mush
brinza cheese
petroleum
redheaded Leah
like a hungry wolf
the word he dreams is
dada
dada ice
dada piano
dada flowers
dada tears
dada pendulum
dada vanilla
dada don quixote
dada humid
dada archipelago
dada pharmacy
dada sexennial

dada dichotomous
dada dichroic
dada dicrotic
dada didactic
dada didelphian
dada diluvial
dada dingdong
the fur of dada stretched out in the sun
dada on a hill old fox old dada
sammy rosenstock alive old exile
got Zurich on my mind
glass toys betwixt the stars with chains
electric flags & posters
"logic is a complication!"
"logic is always wrong!"
cries dada
holy cow
o cube
o hobby horse
the freedom first encountered in
first trip to Zurich
ghosts drunk on energy
they pulled the bells of war down
martyred the cabaret
until it exploded
like yiddish dada in the street
the overture to cheese
o Sammy brother
the sad one of your tribe
you said: disgust
you sat next to the photo of
redheaded Leah
under the axe & clock
your monocle hung from your vest
red life grew distant
in the room where Lenin sat
the walls sang politics to us
his nurse's name was "dada"

so was yours
& sputtered poetry
redbellies laughing thru empty skulls
"my name is Sammy Rosenstock
"Samiro
"is later Tristan Tzara
"I am so sad with life
"I love it
"I am of course Rumanian
"I allow myself to contradict
"I put an owl in a hexagon
"I climb on the stage
"I'm prim
"I'm formal
"I applaud the revolution
"the hands of bandits
"blind worms & dada nightmares
"invade your bowels
"messiahs are passé
"the word we dream is
"dada
"dada sweepeth out
"dada teareth linens
"rips clouds & prayers to shreds
"thou rides on hiccups
"dada has a balcony
"we squat there   pregnant birds
"we shit on thine umbrella
"dada
"dada is against the future
"dada lives
"in fire   wisdom   fear
"—is fear of dada
"like a star?—
"no   like a fish   a plant   the moon
"a metal word
"distorted   boiling
"illumines the urethra

"sixty fingers on each arm
"I am a monster too
"I play with cushions
singing
singing
like hymns of queens
the eye of Lenin
now so wide
pushes the curtains
the chess game opens like a poem
metaphysics of perdition
rules them
tired of the stars
his horse eats colored snakes
o angel horse
on thee rides Hugo Ball
himself an angel horse
here Huelsenbeck & Jung walk
here Arp
here Janco
here kings of Zanzibar
here April nuns
here Tristan Tzara
ghost of Abulafia no ghost
he makes his buttocks jump
like belly of oriental queen
madonna face of Emmy Hennings
a silent fiddle
cuts the room in two
Hugo like a mannikin
at piano
stammers   yodels   farts in rhyme
in lusts of sabbath
—hiccups—
—bowwows—
dusts off the mask of dada
cardboard horsehair leather wire cloth
wears dada collars   dada boots

cothurnus of a bishop
lesbian sardines
ecstatic mice
vanilla derbies
from corners of Cabaret Voltaire
how many kings crow?
how many krazy kittens
cry for you?
how many centuries between
Zurich & Moinesti?
how many grandfathers?
how many clicks before the poem ends?
how much incesticide?
how many accordions to serenade
redheaded Leah?
belated
Lenin dies
brave gymnasts march again
thru workers' suburbs
Stalin's moustache adrift
—o feckless future—
writes Mandelstamm:
"huge laughing
"cockroaches on his lip
"the glimmer of his boot rims
"scum & chicken necks
"half human
"the executions slide across his tongue
"like berries
o revolutions of the fathers
you tease us back to death
pink sands of California
line my coast
saloons & oracles
stemming the tide
can't end it
you are dead
& dada life is growing

from your monocle
ignored   exalted
you lead me to my future
making poems together
flames & tongues we write
like idiots
ballets of sperm
a brain song for the new machine
squadrons of princes pissing in the street
—intensity—
—disgust—
an empty church from which
you drew the drapes back
the face of Jesus on each drape
"on each Jesus was my heart"
you wrote
messiah of stale loaves
of frogs in shoes
god dada
messiahs are passé
there is no greater savior
than this   no eye
so credible
your fart that night was luminous
it stoked the cannons
thruout Europe
in the bus to Amsterdam
in Missouri in Brazil in the Antilles
in a bathrobe
under your bed the shadows massed
like sleeping robbers
the moon became our moon
again o moon
over Moinesti
o moon of tiny exiles
moustaches of antelopes we eat
& cry out "fire"
"water"

interrogate the pope, was arrested & condemned to die, & only escaped after the pope's own death. FRANK (1726–1791), born Yakov Leivich in Podolia, recognized himself as messiah in the fullest sense, followed Sabbatai Zevi into Islam, & from there took the further road to Roman Catholicism. Legends of sensuality surrounded him, tied in with his proclamation of his daughter, Eva, as the female aspect of God (= Shekinah). TZARA (his name means "sad paisano") was born Sammy Rosenstock in Moinesti, Rumania, & was the central poet of Zurich & early Paris Dada, who wrote: "Let every man shout: there is a great negative work of destruction to be done. Sweeping, cleaning. The cleanliness of the individual affirms itself after the state of madness, the aggressive complete madness of a world left in the hands of bandits who vandalize & destroy the centuries. . . . Those strong in words or in strength will survive, for they are quick to defend themselves." His own path went through poetry & communism, & he made no messianic claims.

The other poets included herein are Hannah Weiner, who—like Abulafiia perhaps—sees "words on my forehead, in the air, on other people, on the page"; Osip Mandelstamm, who died in prison, *circa* 1938, after poem that blasted Stalin; & assorted Zurich Dadaists of Cabaret Voltaire.

"avalanche"
a swamp of stars waits
toads squashed flat against
red bellies
at center of a dream
—magnetic eyes—
whose center is a center
& in the center
is another center
& in each center is a center
& a center on each center
centered
centering
composed by centers
like earth
the brain
the passage to other worlds
passage to something sad
lost dada
an old horse rotting in the garden
maneless   waiting
for the full moon
someone leaps into the saddle
rushes after you
exuding light

NOTE TO "ABULAFIA'S CIRCLES"

At conclusion of *Poland/1931* & *A Big Jewish Book*, I was left w
afterimages of largely unresolved messianic figures: historic
mythic. Of these, three appear in the present series: Abrah
Abulafiia, Jacob Frank, & Tristan Tzara. ABULAFIA (1240–*c*.12
was a mystic & poet, whose most developed visual/meditative w
took the form of 200 mandalic circles, made up of letters & wo
He also adopted the name of the angel Raziel, went as messiah